Hurt People ... Hurt People

By William S. Graham

A self – help guide that highlights the parable of trauma, heartache, and pain.

☹

♒♋♍♊♋♌♍♎♏♐♑♒♓♈♉

GRAHAMR WRITINGS LLC
PUBLISHING COMPANY

Hurt People....Hurt People/William S. Graham

ISBN-13: 9781798876541

HURT PEOPLE – HURT PEOPLE

A book that shines a spotlight on the everyday emotions we face. Hurt people – Hurt People focus point is to address anger, disappointment, self – destruction, pain, abandonment, hidden truths, and divine insights.

Throughout my journey of wisdom, I found it to be a great relief to know that hurt is something that a lot of people deal with every day.

Just when you think you are all alone in your broken state of discomfort, here comes someone who understands your pain. I wrote this book to reach out to others with high hopes to heal myself and my friends (you guys are my friends).

Thank you for your time and true patience.
Mr. Williams S. Graham #123781.

"If you hurt someone in life, you hurt yourself in the mirror of reflections.'

Reflection –

we

   see

what

   we

want

   to see

when

   we

look

in the mirror

ACKNOWLEDGEMENTS

Ronald Prye, my dear brother and comrade once said "when you understand what you want out of life, it makes the journey a lot easier to go get it."

I met a few people in my life that I can honestly say I grew from knowing them. Thank you all.

Ronald "Tiger" Prye Marilyn Boyin Prye – My beloved mother Tecarra "Ceasar Lawn" Graham – My brother Evertt M. Harrington – My brother and comrade Chris "C – Mac" Miller – My brother and comrade Damon 'The Nomad' to be better in life. Michael "Spike Mike" Scadden, and Deanna Scadden – I admire your love for each other.

Special thanks to all my kids Jaliyah, Cyprese, Lovely, Essence, Baby Bro, Lil Shugg, Imani.
You guys keep me strong.

Special thanks to Anthony Loudy and John Trujillo – two guys who have shown realness and support when others turned their backs.

Damion Perez – a dear friend and comrade who has a good heart and I'm blessed to call him my friend. Thank you!

Sean Marshall – a brother who gave me insight when I needed it the most. You are a true artist.

Antonio Stancil "Baby Bounce" thank you for struggling with me.

R. I. P. Karkas Graham – My baby brother who told me to keep writing and showing the world my truth.

Robert Bodison "Lil Loko" thank you for being one of the realest guys I have ever met.

Cory Woodard "Lil C" – You are someone who I can say has a heart of gold. Thank you, Home town.
Lester Newton 'Big Les Dawg' thank you for showing me all the game you did.

Eugene Russell – "Lil KB" (thank you for always being my little brother and staying real through all the stuff we went through.

Hova Thomas – Love you big bro.

Permanent Love.

Thank you to the Pepper Family.

Special thanks to Marquita L. Graham, my beloved wife and best friend. You are someone I can honestly say makes life worth living. Love you.

Special thanks to the staff @ D. R. D. C. (you guys are very rare, and that is something I will never forget).
Thank you all.

I wrote this book hoping to free others but found that it freed me as well.

Thank you.

Always remember it pays to be YOU!

Hurt People – Hurt People

October 1st, 1990, I sat on the steps of a group home called Helping Hands, with a blank stare in my eyes.

Looking at an orange horizon before me.

My heart broken into a million pieces as I asked myself a few questions. 'What did I do wrong?', 'why don't my parents want me? Was I one of the misfit toys on an island of broken dreams? Something to be discarded or calmly pushed to the side like a plate of leftover food.

I was confused and broken-hearted to my core.

A seven-year-old with no direction would be the best way to describe me at that point in my life. I say the worst thing for a anyone is not having direction.

This book is dedicated to anyone who has ever been mistreated, overlooked, outcasted, and broken hearted.

But please don't get it twisted by reading this, Hurt People – Hurt people, is not your run of the mill self – help book.

I'm not here to ride the pity train with you. I'm here to show you how to get off that mug.

I truly believe everyone has a purpose in life. Even haters have a purpose.

CHAPTER 1:

Hurt as Well

What is a hater? A person, place, or thing with no general purpose in life, besides preventing you from achieving your goals.

Who can be a hater? Your mother, your father, your aunty, your uncle, your sister, your bald-headed bucktoothed brother, your brown-nosing co-worker who is always switching on you to your boss, your obese baby momma who obviously seems jealous of your new girlfriend and step kids. (Yes, she hates the kids as well). Basically, a hater is anyone who stays in your business more than layers stay in court rooms.

Where can you find a hater?

In your business.

Why do haters hate? Because it's in their nature. Like vultures and buzzards.

When is the best time to dodge a hater?

Every chance you get.

How that we know what a hater is and who can be one, let's move on to another subject. Haters don't get that much attention in any of my books ... sorry.

Trust

Ask yourself who do you trust?

Why do you trust that person?

Now ask yourself who don't you trust?

Why don't you trust that person?

If you could make that person who you don't trust disappear to another world, would you?

Stronger Things

Growing up in the streets, I noticed something about myself (I did not enjoy using harsh drugs.)

I have been round harsh drugs all my life, but never felt tempted to try any of them. A true contradiction walking, seeing how I have sold these name harsh drugs to others. (I know right). But the reason I never did hard drugs stems back to seeing so many people I cared about getting high.

I remember watching my uncle shoot dope into his veins with a dirty needle. His veins were bruised and damaged to the point of no return.

I asked myself who would want to do this to themselves?

My question got answered by my own mother who went to prison for over 20 years behind a drug robbery gone wrong.

This level of traumatic occurrence gave me a sense of hurt that left a stain on my view of using drugs.

For quite some time I even judged people with drug problems.

Looking at them in a certain light that reflected ill – will feelings back to my mother.

It wasn't until I begun taking classes for drugs and alcohol and became a member of P.E.A.K. (Peer Education Adjustment Keepers) which gave me a new light.

I got to know the people behind the drugs and seen their sickness was real. Some of them turned to drugs as a way to cope with the pain they suffered as a child.

Yes, We Did!

They were me in another form of life.

I noticed how within a blink of an eye I could have been one of them.

Honestly, I was one them, a hurt addict.

I begin robbing people as a way of coping with the absent nature of my mother. It became so bad that I no longer cared about the money. Don't get me wrong I knew the money like water, but it was more about the power that I felt when I was in control.

How else would I explain 31 egg, robberies and 9 kidnappings?

I was only 18 years old when I did these things. Not some full-grown man who understands why he does something, but a hurt kid who did not know how to deal with such pain.

Ask yourself what do you have inside of you, buried deep away from the world, that no one knows about?

You probably be shocked to find out what hides inside your heart. (Pain, anger, shock, need, abandonment, and many other things that fester deep in our cores.)

We all drive our cars of hurt on a highway of confusion . . . hoping not to crash.

Forgiveness

I had this one girlfriend.
All she did was get high.
Everywhere we went she would sneak off to get high.
I used to ask her why?
But she had no idea why?
I held her when she was crying
Told her to be strong
Loved her when she was broken
Right or wrong
I was her rock
Her reason to say
Her only good thing in life
From day to day
When people who doubt her . . . I would not
When she would doubt herself
I still gave her a lot
One day out of the blue she got arrested
For drugs and drinking
I visited her in the county
Asked her what was she even thinking?
She just sat there staring into my eyes . . . as if she did not
know me
She was trapped in a world of lost, trying to get free

Chapter 2

Are you being prepared?

THE GREATEST ASSET

The greatest asset of any nation is the spirit of its people, and the greatest danger that can menace any nation is the breakdown of that spirit – the will to win and the courage to work.

George B Cortelyou

We don't typically hold people responsible for their personality traits, but we certainly do so for their habits of character. Russell W. Gough

I never made any excuses for my behavior mainly because I knew better. Like I said I wanted to be the bad guy. I was fascinated by them, as many of us are, that's why we idealized them. We say doing crime is wrong but think about a lie without crime, financially. All the judges, attorneys, officials and any branch of authority – would no longer serve a purpose toward that field of work.

For example, what do detectives do with their lives, career wise, after there is no more crime? What if they've been a detective for 15 to 20 years? Does he or she work at a grocery store? A museum, a book store, a car lot, etc. etc. etc. no matter what they do in life it won't be their passion. Which is kind of weird if you point out how their desire to chase criminals trumps their desire to stop crime altogether.

TWO IN ONE

When Robert Louis Stevenson wrote: 'Dr. Jekyll and Mr. Hyde,' he harped upon a universal string, for every man has intermingled within him the high and the low, the beautiful and the unsightly, the angelic and the bestial, the laughter and the tears, the sunlight and the shadows of life. Every man's life is a battleground where virtue grapples with vileness, where the beacons of conscience seek to vanquish the legions of man's erring nature. Man is a two-fold being in whom the valleys of evil align themselves against the mountains of purity and seek to becloud their summits.

The outcome of this battle in the soul is highly important to the welfare of the individual. Should the lower nature of man emerged victorious from the strife, man will find himself groping in the morasses and midnight of life.

But if his higher nature wins, he will be elevated in spirit to the mountain – peaks of an enriched life, while the sunlight of virtue envelopes him and darkness holds no fears.

Each man may determine within himself where the feet of his spirit shall walk.

Leo Bennell in Sunshine Magazine

RANDOM THOUGHTS

Many people owe the grandeur of their lives to their tremendous difficulties.

Manners are the shadows of virtues, the momentary display of those qualities which our fellow creatures love and respect.

Sydney Smith

Working is more than a way of earning a livelihood, it is a way of keeping one's self – respect.

Those who are out to borrow trouble will find that they have an excellent credit rating.

Money won't buy friends, but ti will get you a higher grade of enemies.

Greed

The pawn shop had a variety of customers that evening. My partner was quite new to this whole robbing lifestyle. Sitting in the passenger seat of the blue Ford Taurus he was quiet, too damn quiet if you ask me. I felt it to be my criminal duty to say something and put his nerves at ease, not to add I didn't want to get my head blow off. 'Look man, you down to this?' The tone in my voice was aggressive, but motivational as well. He just shook his head agreeing with me, 'You ready?' I said it with a hint of laughter in my voice. The owner probably considered himself to be thinking man, seeing how he hired another person to watch his back (Smart but stupid)

10:30pm, the back door revealed to figures existing the pawn shop. I knew this information from my surveillance work I did 3 months previously. My crime partner and I were positioned behind a giant green dumpster waiting for them. In a flash it happened, weapons drawn, we got the jump on them quickly. Eyes the size of saucers could describe their facial expressions, 'Get down!' I shouted. Looking around to see if anyone heard me besides these two jackasses. So-called body guard was a white gentleman with a protruding stomach, a scruffy heard, and a revolver on his hip. The gun was a true relic if I say so myself (I wonder why?) I disarmed the guy as he was lying on his huge stomach.

13

Seeing his demeanor, from what I can tell, he didn't want to die like this – in some dirty, piss filled alley – I understood his sympathies. I told myself when I first started robbing people that my goal was to get money and not hurt people. (I didn't stay true to my oath)

No mercy in my veins, that's how you stay on top in a pirate's world. I took full control of the situation once I knew the known pistol was neutralized. Quickly patting each one down as they laid there 'get up' I said in a firm tone. They both compiled as if they had a choice in the matter. The owner was shaking as he twisted the key inside the lock. Within seconds we all were standing at the back entrance of the door. The owner quickly informed us that he had a guard dog inside his office. (Don't know why he told us that, but he did) nonetheless I moved gracefully through the dark. I was getting a bad vibe from the fat guy, so I bound his feet and hands together real good. The owner was forced into the office where he led the dog into the bathroom area and closed the door. I can still hear the sound of its barking ringing in my ears now. The owner pulled out a metal box . . . it was filled with money and a gold watch. Stuffing it in my cargo pockets I told the owner to move toward the jewelry case. My crime partner handed me the garbage bags as I watched him keep tech over the fat body guard. (A part of me was truly proud as a father would be, very sick I agree). He opened the case and stood to the side, which I thought was cute because it was so amateur hour. A dumb robber would have started grabbing items without concentrating on the pawn shop owner, hands full. I gave him the bags, telling him to fill them up while I held him at gun point. We walked away with about 5 grand in cash, a nest egg of jewels, and about 7 X – boxes, and 6 Play Stations. A pretty nice score for two kids that were so dumb that they didn't know the difference between bread and crumbs. My crime partner had a smile on his face, but I was unsatisfied with the take. I wanted more . . . I was greedy.

JUDGE

Humble Pie

She said "be more humble"
I thought to myself –
maybe this is true
But I do feel humble
Humble when I look at you
Seriously though
I wonder about your journey
All the things you have been through
All the things that made you blue
All the things that made you . . . you

I was more humbled once
On the front porch –
waiting on my dad to show up
He never did
I had to grow up
But I lost my sense of being humble
Afraid of being hurt again
Heart the color of cherry pie
I was even more humble . . . until I seen her black eye
My uncle hit my aunt
I wanted to die
I had to cry
Watching him from the car as we left the only home I have
ever known
I said to myself do not cry anymore
Do not feel pain

Do not be humble
Humble feels the same
as being that helpless kid
The one who did nothing
but watched
and cried

"I wrote this poem to paint a picture how a kid can grow up with pain in their heart from the things that occur in their lives. As a child I found myself asking why life had to be so complex, but as I grew up I begin to see that life is a struggle – every day we must continue to fight for the things we love and hold dear to our hearts.

I am working on being more humble, or should I say being more thoughtful of others and myself . . . thank you"

What I Know

I know what it feels like when your life seems as if you are walking on a dead-end road. Trying to find purpose, passion, or peace. You tell yourself (what I would do for a little spark). Anything will do to combat the drowning stages of boredom.

Before I started writing and working out daily I was in the same boat, I call this the wandering stage,
House moms usually get it after 10 continuous years of washing clothes, cooking food, cleaning the house, and a slew of other things to keep your mind off what you always wanted to do . . . jump out of a plane head first (just kidding, maybe!)

Anyway, I recall sitting in my prison cell watching the officer pass out mail, asking myself why don't I feel important?

Because I wasn't at the time. I didn't have anything going on, I was stupid, gang banger, with limited education and jaded view of the world. Feeling as the world owed me something.

Rule number one: the world does not owe you anything (dog eat dog remember). The quicker you discover that the better off you will be, trust me.

Writing gave me that outlet I was searching for; a state of being to be proud about. I discovered the power of the pen, truthfully it gave me a rush, and that's saying a lot coming from a guy who use to ran up in banks with a ski mask on his face.

I can't say what your purpose is or may be, but I do know you – everyone has one. You just have to find it . . . or let it find you (whichever one comes first). Good Medicine.

Beware of the candy-coated flavoring.

Photo by Gabriel Matula on Unsplash

Then I noticed how people who have
been hurt, tend to hurt others as well.

Hurt People – Hurt People

Have you ever felt you deserved a promotion, and did not receive it? Did you poke your lip out, sitting in the corner sulking?

Or did you get upset and take your anger out on someone else?

As we take a long look at the daily newspaper, well see the effects of being hurt/misunderstand.
Something we all search for, (A reflection of self)

THE DIFFERENCE

While removing finger smudges from the different doors in the house, mother asked, 'Joan, are you the little girl who always puts your dirty fingers on the door?'

'Oh, no, Mother,' replied the little girl, 'they can't be my fingerprints – I always kick the doors open!'

FRIENDSHIP

Hurt People – Hurt People

Nicholas Pachecs AKA Finger once told me 'it is what it is, and it will be what it will be ~ but never again will it be what it was.'

True friendship comes at a price man people wouldn't dare pay. The cost is too high to bare.

Rony Aktins also knows as 'Big 40 oz' is a stand wo guy and a great friend.

Feeling Good

Name five things that bring you joy or make yo feel good, not counting sex, drugs, eating, sleeping or making money. Think of some things that make you laugh or maybe cry.

Once you have your list check one thing on your list that brings you the most joy (do not say your kids, or church please don't)

Do the first thing that brings you joy, then two weeks later do the second thing on your list, then the 3rd, and so on and so on until you get to the 5th.

By the time you get to the last thing you should be feeling a little better, if not call Dr. Phil and tell him you need real help cause I failed you. Free your mind.

Feeling good is no secret, it is a place of peace that one must find and keep (hold sacred). Do not let others know where your state of peace resides – they want a piece of your peace.

How you look – how you feel + how you think = smiley faces

I had many barbers in my life time, but only two comes to mind when I say the word best. (What?!)

I acknowledge the haters will disagree but I'm just being honest – please do not shoot me.

Drum roll please: "and the awards go to Damon Davis, and Michael E. Harrington.

Both of these gentlemen cut my hair just the way I liked it. I have a funny looking head, and everyone knows it. But these two artists have/possess the proper skill to overcome this, that my friends, is what I call talent.

If you look good . . . you feel good – plain bagel.

WORTH REMEMBERING

If we cannot get all we want, we should be thankful we don't get all we deserve.

He is not only idle who does nothing, but he is idle who might be better employed.

Little minds are wounded by little things.

Chapter 4

of

UNIQUE

Time

Personal values: You start working for this elite company which starts your salary off at 40 dollars per hr.
Your rent is due, your child is sick, and you are on parole.

After 6 months of working there you discover the company is stealing money from the public – what do you do?

REALISM

Your best friend is dying in 6 months, but you can't tell them because if you do your child will die instantly. What would you do?

"We are made by the likes of our conditions and broken by the spoils of our comforts."

—William Graham

What is realism to you?

I own my mind. I give my heart. I praise my soul. I forgive my mistakes. I protect my thoughts. I watch my actions. I feel my pain. I understand my past. I respect my elders. I honor my family – real family. I remember my words. I love my growth. I withstand my addictions. I write my passions. I know myself. Do you?

Your girlfriend throws up at a company party. Your boss is a true germicidal maniac who says something disrespectful about her to you, unaware that she is your girl – friend. Later on that night, your girl – friend ask you if she made a good first impression on your boss.

What do you tell her?

And do you ever tell your boss that was your girl – friend who threw up at his party?

ENCOURAGEMENT

Every morning the sun rises, every spring the flowers bloom, every night the Great Dipper is just where it is supposed to be, most parents love their children, 98 per cent of your youngsters are not delinquents, most promises are faithfully kept, and there is will far more love than hate in the world, in spite of all the television and newspaper headlines.

Pana (III), News - Palladium

32

The Girl Down the Hall

Her screams echo off the walls
For help she calls
We all hear her, but no one wants to meddle in their business . . . to the ground she falls
Treated like a dog
Hogs have it better
Maybe we think to small
Or maybe we only stand tall on the shoulders of those who are fearless . . . unlike us
Neglecting the girl down the hall
One day I seen her crawl
I dropped my head and said awe
I dropped my head and said awe
As if my sympathy would pick her up and wipe her bloody nose, ripped clothes, and everything exposed
I did not know
Until we no longer hear the screams
Our help no longer needed
 She lays there dead in the hallway
On our faces you can read it
A look of shame for the girl down the hall

'The balance of being yourself is judged by your actions and thoughts'

When I first wrote this piece, it touched me to see how deep my mind could expand. To know this happens every day and still ask myself how many people walk by and do nothing? not saying I'm some kind of super hero or anything like that, I just believe that cowards hold bags of sand in their pants. Personally, I cannot sit back and watch a woman get her brains best in y a man, but don't get me wrong woman have first too, and I also believe in keeping your hands to yourself. (message)

BUSINESS CHARACTER

What a business stands for will never be anything different from what its people stand for. the respect it is held in will be determined by the respect they command as individuals and as a team. Do they have, and do they keep on getting, the knowledge they require for the job they are called on to do? Do they have the needs of the public and the good of the country deeply at heart? Can they always be relied on? Will they walk the second mile? Are they ceaselessly driving for excellence – for high quality – for performance that will astonish people because it si so good? Do they base their decisions and actions on what they earnestly believe is right for the long run, rather than on consideration s of temporary advantage?

Frederick R. Kappel, Chairman of the Board, American Telephone and Telegraph Company

35

Emotion

As we know, in many different ways, venting your distress to others is a very healthy experience.

Life deals us all kind of hands, some are good, while some we consider bad. But the growth we attain from these losses are theoretically what makes us strong.

Someone once vented this passage to me over the loss of her beloved father passing away. May he rest in peace.

I'm just beside myself. Trying to keep my temper of bay. Feeling overwhelmed and slightly disheveled. I don't really know if I have any strength left in me. All this pain, hurt, disappointment. I don't think I can cry anymore. I'm filled with hope and hatred. I just want my daddy to get well. I want my boss to die. I just can't take it. I love my job, but I hate how things are going. I have a great support system and I should be happy, but the disdain I feel for humans and humanity is so much greater than the hope I hold in my heart. I'm mad at everyone yet again for the way things have worked out! The cards I've been dealt! Paying the game f life and trying to live is just not real. It can't be done. Some folks, their pain and unrest is masked. I wear it on my face. The stupid question 'are you okay?' Makes me want to punch people in the face. No, I', not okay! No. I don't 'feel' better. I'm angry! I'm sad! I'm hurt and wounded. I just can't! I want to just drop kick everyone! Here is not peace for me. I've given up! I can't fight anymore! I have no fight left in me. How am I to move on from this? How does one heat? How do I stop being angry? Do I just told and walk away? Or do I just continue to muddle through this pointless ass life. Full of debt and disappointment!!!

I'm just venting my sheer frustration with life right now! No one rent to talk to no one to hold me when I cry. No one who understands.

Believe

I didn't want to know the future – she told me anyway
When I was going to die
What a day
The actual day I was going to die
I couldn't believe it
Why?
I didn't want to die
Tears in my eyes
She said "don't cry".

I got made
Stood up
She said, "please sit down!"
I didn't want to
Knocking her table over as I walked out
Her face was stone
Everything was different now
Food tasted better
Time was timeless
Nature was beautiful
I closed my eyes to see my future in front of me
I had to live
My heart pounded harder
She was wrong
Death would have to wait for me
I didn't want to know the future – she told me anyway
Crystal clear days

Sometimes it is best not knowing what the future has in store for us. I used to spend a large amount of my time trying to change or effect what the future had in store for me.

Now I live by a different creed – one that does not stress me out or demand I go bald before I reach my late 50s.
Someone once told me (worry is like the beach, always willing to get in your shorts and stress you out)

FUN

When was the last time you had some real fun? Think about it, I mean real non-mobile fun. Do you even remember?

Life is too short not to have fun or enjoy everything it has in store for us.

Today buy a bag of water balloons and fill them up with water. Go home, trick your love ones outside, and bomb their asses into the stone ages. Trust that you will have some real fun. Laugh and enjoy the fact that life is truly dear – make sure you tell them you love them from your heart.

"Never forget you only live once . . . Enjoy it!"

POWER

Tomorrow when you wake up you discover you have developed a special power.
The power to transform into anyone you desire to be. First who would you transform in to?
And secondly what would you do with your newly profound power?

"Consider what a flower has to endure and tell me how hard life is. Consider what a butterfly goes through and tell me I cannot change"

Chapter 5
of

A RECIPE FOR TOMORROW

Untied

My heart is broken

Left open

Unspoken words to say

Inside

My heart is an ocean

Left open

Each and everyday

Inside

I play with such thoughts

In my mind I play

In my heart

Deep in my heart

I stay

Untied

At bay

Afraid

To say

I'm trapped in my own fray   **Untied**

A Baby Step

All these year later
Hate runs deep still
Hidden agendas coming to surface
How do we really feel?
Should we kill everything
Let everything die
Say we sorry between clenched teeth
Then ask why?
The next generation destroys themselves
With a pair of bloody hands to deny
Burning candles
Holding hands
The tears we cry
Do we act our way through acting school?
Or do we even try?
I believe its all a lie
Unconvinced on humanity's shy baby steps
and closed eyes.

THE WISE MEN

That which the fool does in the end the wise man does in the beginning.

R. C. Trench

Money and Music

Both give you a sense of power

Growing up I was privileged to fully understand the arches of money and music. They both gave me a sense of joy in my life. Crazy times as I remember my first job (a tobacco field) taught me a lot. Five hour shifts in the searching heat made us respect a tall glass of water. The work was hard, but it gave us younger guys a strong sense of independence. 30 dollars a day was good money for a 14-year-old back then. Not to add it fell truly liberating dancing to my music and counting my money in my room. I brought me some brand-new sneakers and some candy with my first check. I was free back then, not a care in the world, so innocent. I had a quote on my wall back then and I smile at the thought of it today "whatever brings you comfort wares your soul". They call them creature comforts, and if you have one cherish it. Never forget why these things bring you joy – solace.

Challenge

During my high school days, I learned a life lesson which altered my thinking process. My high school took football pretty serious at the time. Everything was practice and good grades. Practice and good grades, practice and good grades. Every day I heard this over and over again. Favorite saying of Coach Anderson "if you do not understand what I am saying then this is not the football team for you". You see

Coach Anderson had a very unique way of getting his point across to his players, and he knew it was effective by the number of wins he had on his record over the years. I remember playing this rival team one year, who instantly became our thorn in our sides.

They were so arrogant it made my skin crawl every time I walked through their halls to enter the field.

I even recall the "boooo, boooo, boooo" I use to get looking up in the stands to see mothers and washed up fathers glaring at me with darting eyes. Aware that I was the one who could ruin their spoils of victory. I took pleasure in doing that every year.
Pop!

The ball flew in the air like a knife cutting through butter. I looked up to see the force of their layers marching toward us. A stampede of destruction.

We did not panic, as we knew Coach Anderson prepared us battle enough to win the game.

Anyway, we won the game, but I lost the balance of lessons that Coach Anderson was trying to teach us. Refusing to shake their hands made Coach Anderson mad . . . I knew it.

My Baby Brother

Walk like me . . . talk like me . . . only one year apart.

Kind as a mouse . . . with a lion's heart

Smile from ear to ear . . . middle finger to the world

Always said I player . . .he only loved one girl

Talent beyond your imagination . . . a rare gift indeed

Spoke what he felt . . . wore his heart on his sleeve

He sure did love himself some me though

Dreams about becoming a rapper

We would grow up to be

Football game and late-night clubs

Sweet candy and potato chips for dinner

That boy could always grub

Like our Pitbull puppies that froze in the cold

I sit here dear brother (missing you from my soul)

Never had any kids, but you loved my kids to death

Even when you had nothing to give thee

You gave them what you had left

6 months to live

My eyes cried rapidly red

Even prayed to our heavenly Father

Asking him to take me instead

But he did not little brother

He chose you

An angel with rough edges, what was I supposed to do?

What will I do?

My baby brother and best friend is gone

Even in a room full of people

I still feel all alone....without my baby brother

Dedicated to Shay T. & K. Graham, RIP

THE DOUBTER

ACHIEVEMENT

What are you waiting for? A train or some magical school bus to come pick you up and carry you to a land of greatness? You have to work hard at your dreams if you want them to come true. No short cuts. No putting it in some other persons hands, hoping it gets done the way you see it in your mind. Stop looking out the window of life, go down stairs, open the door, and take a deep breath. That is living life with no regrets my friends.

Understand that life is short, and time is beautiful. Within a blink of an eye it could be over. Sad but true.
Ambition is not sold at the local market down the street, or in some place far away from here. You have to want it so bad that you make it happen.

Repeat after me: I deserve greatness.

I am ready to accept my dreams.

I am not afraid to grow from my mistakes.

I will not let anything stop me from achieving my goals.

I will succeed.

I know my path and I walk it without judgment.

I believe.

The moment I became an author my whole life changed. I knew why I wanted to write … I think. Not! I take that back. At first, I did not know why? I just know I had a lot of things to say and felt as if no one was listening to me. It made me mad. Until I discovered the old paper and pen. The oldest living tool of venting, if you do not count the south.

I have a box of rejection letters that I keep under my bed for the purpose of thought. Letting me know to always cherish my art. But the kicker here is I did not let these letters of rejection break my spirits. I told myself I'm going to write no matter what. I could care less if anyone feels different about that. Even till this day I write what I feel, and not what I believe will make people happy.

I put my first 5 books out for free, what!!!
That is right, for free!
Why? Because I was free when I did it. Meaning I did not free the books – they freed me.

Never give up!

Chapter 6
of

STRENGTH
IN NUMBERS

Change

"Baby I don't think you know how to change"

Her words bounced off the walls and stuck in my brain like
(Damn)
Was she serious?

Hell, I even got curious
Asking myself . . .what remains?

After I have played all the games and forgot the names,
What remains?

Deep in my core I thought about this comment
It bothered me
Worried me sickly
I said to myself (she doesn't know me, I can change if I
wanted to ... I just need time)
Or maybe a sign

"Like this one"
No not like that
You know a sign from God

Yeah that will set me straight
That will definitely get me right
When I looked up it had become night
I said "I will change in the morning"

Good night.

"Change is a road trip not a bear run"

"Your days, your months, your years should never be the same if you want to see true growth"

"Everyone has a tomorrow, go get it"

> There's so much good in the worst of us, and so much bad in the best of us, that it's hard to tell which one of us ought to reform

Remote Control Your Life

Think about your life as a remote controller. First you need a working set of batteries right, or some kind of charge. What charges you up? What motivates you?

Your kids? Your dreams? Freedom? Legacy? etc. etc. These things are very vital in the stages of controlling your life.

Alright once you have your working batteries, you have to have the courage to turn on the power button. The power button is your consciousness which governs your drive to achieve greater things in life.

The channel buttons control what you are viewing the content of what draws your attention. Are you a drama freak? Do you fiend for action in your life? Do you still have haunting hope dreams floating around your head?

Everything you watch has a purpose in your life. Take me for an example: I love watching the show 'The Walking Dead'. It is a great show to me. But also understand I have a side of me that longs to see what would happen if the world ended. I like to see who people transforms into when faced with a make or break situation.

Anyway, the volume buttons control what you hear.
The volume buttons are very important in controlling your life. Simply because the message you receive is the one that

matters the most. (If you are putting good advice on mute you have a big problem)

Picture setting: Standards – custom – vivid
Zoom
Favorites

Rewind. How many of us rewind our lives; playing the same part of the movie over and over again. Refusing to move on from our favorite scenes.

Some lessons in life need to be rewound in order to fully grasp the content and learn but be careful. If we get stuck in rewinding our lives, we will move on to the next level of our lies.

Fast forward: Do not be too eager to fast forward past things that you need to take in. (No matter if you like what you see or not . . . take it all in)

I believe you get the picture when I say your life is yours to live. Understand that by controlling your life you will gain a new profound sense of purpose. A purpose that will help you grow beyond the day to day lessons that might be bestowed upon you.

"If you do not control your life someone will control it for you"

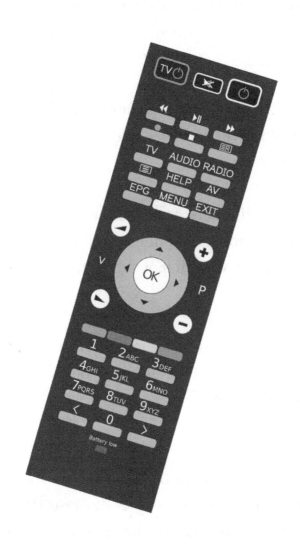

Patience

In recent years I have noticed a spike in road rage incidents in our country. People are losing their ever-loving minds while behind the wheel of their cars.

The highways and byways have become more dangerous than ever, forcing us to ask what is the problem?

Is it patience?

Have we become so spoiled in our self-centered world of rush and flush that we do not see ourselves in the mirror?

"In a hurry to go nowhere fast" is what my grandmother used to say.

Patience is something we must continue to respect. We feel a giant wave of entitlement will shackle us down and prevent us from missing something dear.

Sadly, do I say only in our minds do we feel restless or better yet impatient in life. Trust me when is ay you are not missing anything special, or maybe you are just crazy as hell.

"Grow fond of breaking bad habits before they grow fond of breaking you"

Fear and Despair

At the age of nine years old I stood in front of the entire student body class and read a poem I wrote.

My teacher put me up to it, well actually, she bribed me with candy. (I was so weak back then)
Anyway, picture me standing there with a thousand sweat beads on my forehead reading a poem about God knows what!

Scared as hell. Looking crazy as a road lizard.
Trying not to stutter. That was the moment I knew I feared public speaking.

I believe fear holds us at bay sometimes. Telling us we are not good enough to be as we are. When truthfully, we are stronger than what we appear to be.

I overcame my fear of public speaking throughout the years. Now you would not believe that is my main focus in life. Speaking to inmates about change and evaluation is my true love. At the state of my past fear I reflect how someone who thought they could not read a simple poem is now connecting with guys from all walks of life.

Do not allow fear to run your life. Take charge of your fear, using it to empower you instead of crippling you.
Think about what you fear and tell yourself 'I can do this!'

Say it louder 'I can do this!'

It is just that simple. Do not think it is – know it is.

I Just Want To Grow Old

said the little boy
trapped in a gang zone
Sad to say, but he doesn't belong to either side
A small grain of sand
trapped in the tide
His hurt he hides
 Schools are useless
besides who can think when bullets ricochet so ruthless?
The sun never come out
He remembers every kid that never made it out
(Only if Superman was real he says)
Imagination faded
With expectation of his dad who died
Candy lost its taste
A smile was replaced with no trace of hope
Junkies in the alley ways
- smoking dope
Shooting it as well
and the pushers shoot for it
The mayor turns his head to the left
Acting as if he doesn't know it
His mother doesn't show it (love)
Her love is for a bag of white pleasure
Promising to do better
He hears her words but sees her actions in motion
Holding pain in the pit of his soul
He mumbles 'I just want to grow old'

A cold apartment, an empty stomach, bad plumbing, and no
lights outside
no rights
Bullets fly throughout the night
At night
he dreams of a world elsewhere from this
No gang banging
No mothers shooting dope
No kids having kids
No fathers going to court
No police officers locking people up for sport
He says
with a clear voice
bravely and bold
"Forgive me for being so selfish, I just want to grow old"

I wrote this piece for all the kids that feel trapped behind
gang lines, which prevent them from having normal
childhoods like me now. They are hurt by their environment
and the people who make selfish decisions every day.
As we stare in the eyes of all the little kids who suffer this
curse we must ask ourselves (Do we really care?)

Hurt People – Hurt People

Honesty

As a child I was not a very honest person. I lied all the time. It felt good lying to others on a daily basis. To be frank with you I can recall only trusting one person in my early childhood. Tecarra Lee Graham. My older brother, and road dawg to the end. We used to lie for each other, he taught me the buddy system in the art of lying. I studied villains on TV. Solely to be better at tricking others and lying.

As I grew in life there was no life changing experience that made me stop lying, I just woke u one day and said I sick of lying. It was that simple. I just got bored. I wanted a different path. I stopped lying to people.

But here's the funny part about an ex-liar. I can tell when other people are lying to me. You should see how I look at them as I listen to their best lie (saying to myself) is this the beat eggs hour, because this is the worst lie I have ever heard.

I do not mind though, everyone has their dreams right.

"The truth will set you free!"

Whomever wrote that must have been a great liar, and we all know why I blushingly say.

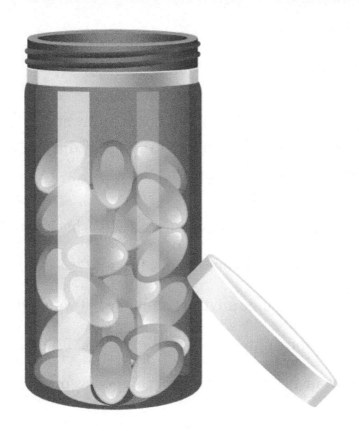

Change

I had a lot of precious people taking from me in my childhood. I begin developing a sense of hate in my heard. I loss even more as a young adult, it was very painfully – the hate grew more intensely. I had so many questions to ask God – I wanted everyone to feel my despair. It wasn't fair I told myself – over and over again I tried to heal my heard. Nothing changed.

Pictures

Digging through a slew of old boxes in my attic, I found an old picture of myself with a lot to say. 'why did you wear that stupid plaid shirt to school that day?'

'Why didn't you take school more serious back then?'

'Do you miss any of your old girl friends?'

'If you could change anything in life, what would it be?'

'Are you happy now?'

'Do all your future pictures look as good as mine?'

The Return

If home was in the heart, I would be lost in the dark

Left behind by the person I love so much

Trapped in an image of you and his lust

Saying to myself 'what happen to us?'

Thank you for showing me the way of trust

Destroyed perfection with one touch – I guess heat of

passion beat you to the punch

Only to take away from the special love we shared

I haunted by the one thing I've always feared

But I must thank you

You did what no other person could do

Brought back a player and buried a love that was true

The Gate of life

It sits there quietly

Regulating the passage of life

Unmoved by our social gathering

A sing

Reading 10,000 volts per person

Enough to run a small town combined

And yes! They're all working

Seeing them go home with a big smile

Watching them come back with a bigger frown

It didn't say a single word out loud

But we know it was calling us clowns

Laughing as hard as 10 years ago

Funny how we didn't see the humor

Weighing on our hearts and minds all day long

Like the effect of a tumor

Or maybe it's just a rumor

And there's no such thing as having to pay the price

Maybe I'm just lying to the younger generation when I say

There's over 1.9 million people, as we speak, living behind the gate of life.

You Find Out Who Your Friends Are

When you need their love it's always there

Not because they want something from you

But because they simply care

How dare you stare into my eyes and tell me nothing but

lies,

Didn't our friendship ties mean anything to you?

Or was it just something to do?

As the times passed by between me and you

I love you from my soul

That's why I'm asking

Why aren't you the person who use to love me?

Why aren't you the beautiful angel that you to be?

Like a butterfly

I've watched you fly free

And wondered what did you see?

Was it a clear blue sky or the shiny starts?

When you're stuck on the ground

That's when you find out who your friends are

Nothing

Under time

We move

Cool

Breathing deeply

Lost

But never found

Perfect little angels

Heavenly bound

A message

In blue ink

Sticking to your soul

Are you open?

I blink

A spoon full of this

Like a star

Brightness your name

It's hard

To see the sky

From, behind a wall

Of shame

Brick by brick

We laugh and claim

Restricted

If the world is round

I am a box

People constantly move around me

I sit and watch

Removed from life distant from light

Darkness within myself

Becomes my sight

Noting owned

Not even a price

Chains on my winds

Delay my flight

Bound to the ground

Deaf to sound

Lost at heart

No longer found

Sad to say

my word is not round,

I'm restricted now

Chapter 7
of

STRATEGY

Beauty

The idea of beauty in our modern-day society is getting an overdue takeover. We are starting to see with true eyes, how beauty has many faces to call home, and giving truth to our future generations to come.

Most kids nowadays take body shaming to another level – committing suicide to combat not feeling beautiful enough. Walking around school balls feeling unaccepted by their peers and the world.

The moment we call ourselves putting a standard on something as complex as beauty, it is a grave down fall in our society. Beauty is a rare entity. Something we must keep a watchful eye on in order to have a grand perspective. Standards are not at a certain level, forcing us to jump through hoops to meet such a quota. But what happens when we do not measure up to a standard that seems to be forever changing?

As a young man full of ambition and blind vigor, I never really noticed how much pressure people put on young girls. Forcing them to evaluate themselves or place themselves in superficial categories (the pretty girls, the poor girls, the strong girls, the rich girls, the smart girls, the ugly girls, and the weird girls etc. etc. etc.)

This cycle continues, with each title adding another level of pressure to the complex element that is true beauty.

Like seriously, who defines beauty in our society? The magazines we worship and match off the shelves? The same magazines that tell us not to be normal and relax in our on comfortable skins. Here's a funny fact: think about all the beautiful artifacts we have in our world. All the landscapes that demand a state of awe. (The Hoover Dam, Tag Mahan, Angkor Watt, Golden Gate Bridge, Eiffel Tower and International space station are all different in their own way, but beautiful.) Nonetheless, we as humans, try our best to destroy them or steal away their essence.

POPULARITY

THE OYSTER AND THE EAGLE

When God made the oyster, He guaranteed him absolute economic and social security. He built the oyster a house, a shell to protect him from his enemies. When hungry, the oyster simply opens up his shell and the food rushes in. but when God made the eagle, He said, 'The blue sky is the limit. Go build your own house, 'And the eagle went out and built his house on the highest mountain crag, where storms threaten him every day. For food, he flies through miles of rain and snow and wind. The eagle, and not the oyster, is the emblem of America.

The Word Victim

At time we find ourselves asking why we have to go through certain obstacles in life to seek happiness.

Unaware of the growth we attain when overcoming such obstacles in our lives.

For example: have you ever wanted to succeed at something you were passionate about? No matter how hard you tried to accomplish your goal, it just seemed to be out of your grasp. But you keep trying no matter what. One day you overcome your obstacle or attain your goal. Imagine the feeling you feel inside your heart. The feeling of knowing you can conquer your goals.

'The greatest of faults is to be conscious of none' – Thomas Carlyle

Once I got back to the foster home I saw how much had changed. Two of my close friends were gone – passed off by the state. My bunk bed was occupied by a red headed kid who seemed to be running things now. At first, I watched him operate under bumptious measurements – pushing people around and using his size to intimidate others. I hated bullies. One of my favorite things in the foster homes was the breakfast cereal that they use to give us. It was all we could eat. As I sat there watching the red headed bully collect his rations from all the other little kids, I couldn't help but laugh.

He was doing such a great job convincing everyone he was a tough guy. Then one day he made a big mistake.
He picked on the wrong kid.

Chad Nickerson was a small frame white kid who did puzzles and had the funniest laugh that I had ever heard. He didn't start any trouble, being a very shy kid, in the foster home.

> If you love life, don't waste time for time is what life is made up of.
> – Bruce Lee

I, on the other hand was like a Cayman waiting in shallow waters. It happened on a normal day. I walked in the open bay area to see the red headed kid with his finger in Chad's face. I bolted into action like some kind of super hero. Pushing his finger away with a quick snap. The red headed kid's face turned the color of a jug of koolaid. He looked at me as if my actions were on unlawful thing. I stepped back with a quick movement, preparing myself for a fight. My eyes were darting inside my head, which promoted a sense of challenge to him. He didn't bite down on the well-prepared bait that I had waiting for him. Instead he chose to take a rain check on my idea of his demise.

Our show down took place later that night in the common bathroom area. I was leaving the bathroom and seen a right fish flying over someone's shoulder. I dodged it with one step, and quickly countered with two punches of my won. He was not prepared for my quickness. Both of my punches landed on the bridge of his nose. He fell backwards from the impact. All the other boys cheered me on as I kicked him. I felt powerful to show him that I was the baddest in the land.

Even though I labeled it as a good deed for my friend, I can honestly say it was more for me. More for my own sense of showing everyone I was strong. I was bad. I was bold. But mostly importantly I wanted to show everyone I was no one's victim.

Prison

18 – 32 and running is the best way to describe my prison experience. I walked in the state penitentiary a young number among giants. The good thing I had on my side was I was raised in the south (North Carolina, South Carolina which instilled respect and a raw sense of thinking ahead.

None the less I was your average hard headed, selfish, hot tempered, and unbelievably cocky knuckle head boy.

They say people in prison are wired a little different than everyone else.

I do not fully agree with that simply because on one side you have the view of the public who see us as animals vs. the people who see us being confused animals (just kidding) but you see where I am going with this right.

At one point in time people serving time were considered the caveman and cavewomen, but all that has changed would you agree. Nowadays for the greater sense of thought, prison has evolved beyond the public if you ask me.

But I question what is it that makes prison such an allure? What makes it the place to be?

Almost like a social club for the misfit toys in some odd way of putting it.

Is it in our hearts and minds do we define ourselves trapped behind a glass of our own thoughts or are we satisfied with the conditions of a controlled life.

Socrates said 'everyone is a prison until they start asking questions and looking for answers'

So, my question to you would be simple: what are you looking for?

Could you imagine being a prisoner to eternity. You could never rest in peace. 5000 years old. Everything you see would be a copy of something that happened over and over again. Nothing would shock you but death, and even then, you might welcome it only to see something new.
How would you feel about humans?

Flaws are something we learn events are something we create -

Forgive Yourself first

Christmas

"Due to the snow storm all bus routes have been delayed definitely"

'What!' 'But it's Christmas Eve!'

"I'm sorry sir ... I truly am, but all the roads are closed at the moment!"

'So, what are we supposed to do? Sleep here for the night ... its cold in here!'

"Unfortunately, sir we're all layed in tonight, feel free to help yourself to our vending machines and complimentary coffee Merry Christmas."

Valentine's Day

In 5th grade I was in love with my teacher. She was beautiful

The kind of beauty that haunts the soul.

I thought about her all day – even when I went home.

He clothes always seem to match her eyes in some odd way.

She was perfect, perfect for me. Her birthday was on

Valentine's Day

I gave her a card with a heart on the front. She got married

to her high school sweet heart a month later.

- Janitors –

Smoking cigarettes in the bathroom – my best friend passed

it to me.

I hit it hard and started coughing instantly, too loud. The

principal heard us walking y – we got caught red handed.

Splash, splash, splash – now we have to mop the floor while

the janitors laugh at us ...

This is my girlfriend

Dr. Such and Such

you pretend

a wishy – washy grin

Saying it was good seeing him again then

(chocolate)

Consolation prize . . . for the loser.

Chapter 8

of

FAULT

Hunger Strike

I went on a hunger strike once. Grounded to my room for
Having bad grades. My mom said stay in there and study
until you pick your grades up. 6.00pm – everyone crowded
around the dinner table. I didn't show up. Then next night
she cooked all my favorite foods – I broke instantly.

Don't Be A Sore Loser

Especially when you see your ex-out with someone else

Maybe at the movies

Or a dinner party

You take a seat in the back

Big shades on watching them

They laugh together

Giving you a salty discharge taste in your mouth

You say 'they're not happy;

Remembering all the opportunities you had

Slowly the clock begins to tick away

you say to yourself

I need a closer look

acting skill

You walk pass "hey!"

blah, blah, blah, blah – how you been?

Blah, blah, blah who's this?

Pocket Lint

My two favorite uncles never talk to each other.

They hate each other with a true passion. My mom said they haven't spoken in over ten years. Grandma use to call them oil and water – they never mixed. The curious nephew I am, asked both my uncles the same questions. Why don't you guys talk? And what prompted this silence? They both blew me off like pocket lint, and still don't talk – 15 years and counting.

Comic book villains

The joker laughed hysterically as he told me a joke.

'A man walks into a jewelry store with a gun and says to the clerk give me all the precious stones;

I listened intently as he continued

'The clerk reached behind the counter pulled out 2 even bigger guns and shot the guy in both knee caps, saying 'this is the last jewelry store you'll walk in.'

Self – knowledge

Who are you? It is a question that many never ask themselves.

Who am I? Am a football player? A family man? A convict? A politician? A teacher? A nurse? An author . . . A food service worker? Or whatever.

I believe we hang sings around our necks for the world to see. Telling ourselves that we are what we do, when in fact we are not. I believe we think our job is who we are.

Have you ever met a doctor who said 'I hate introducing myself as Dr. Such and Such?'

The answer is NO!

They love it, and we as the world have grown to love hearing them say it to us. Not that a doctor should not be proud, but you understand what I am trying to say hear.

In all small talk I simply say this – you are not your job.

Alright, try this. Find a mirror and look deeply into it. Ask yourself the questions: Who am I?

When you do this do not try to win a popularity contest with yourself. Just tell it like it is. Then after you finish with yourself, go ask someone who you know does not like you and them what they think of you? I know I am asking for a lot in asking you to do that, but if you truthfully want to grow you will do it.

Being honest with ourselves is the first stage of finding out who we really are? Remember flattery is always wet and slippery . . . it is like that for a reason.

Mirror, Mirror on the wall . . .
You know the rest.

Trust

As we take along look at trust, its best to ask ourselves – what is trust?

Trust is the power to believe in someone or something you deem reliable. For example: when you're walking down the street on a normal day, you trust that he ground will not cave in or give away under your day, you trust that he ground will not cave in or give away under your feet right! That's trust. But what if you were driving in your car on a normal day, and out of nowhere a sink hole appears in your that. Say you drove into it and were injured badly. How would you feel about trusting the pavement from that point on? Kind of shaky I'm guessing. Who would you blame? Would you fault the city? Would you blame God? Or would you chalk it up to a series of unfortunate events? I trust you would be honest with yourself.

Reliance

Who do you rely on in your daily life? Do you rely on your family members? How about this, do you feel that you can rely on yourself? Do you have confidence in your job occupation? Do you empower yourself to overcome your daily obstacles?

Recently I had a conversation with my son about helping his mom out around the house. He apparently had been neglecting his daily chores to go outside and play with his friends. I asked him a question that I could tell threw him for a loop. I said "son, if your mother was sick and dying and depended on you to take care of the house hold, would you be able to do that?" with honor in his eyes and a level of strength in his voice – he calmly stated, "yes dad I would be able to do that".

After hearing the pride and conviction in his words, I couldn't help but share a story with him. I told him a lady by the name of Ms. Mayberry, who despite her older age took it upon herself to get temporary custody over my older brother and me. Ms. Mayberry was my angel and I truly would have done anything for her. I told my son how thankful I was for her act of kindness that I wash dishes and cleansed the whole kitchen by myself. I learned how to mow the lawn, which was odd for me, seeing how I had never ever lived in a house before or had a yard. I washed clothes and folded them up as neatly as possible. After telling him about all the things I enjoyed doing around the house for her, I also let him know that I also attended school and earned good grades. Sadly though, Ms. Mayberry had to send us back to the foster home due to her having a terminal cancer and did not want my brother and me to witness her decline. The puzzling look, on my son's face informed me he did not fully grasp the effects of my story. I could tell he felt bad about Ms. Mayberry passing away, but he did not comprehend the effects of my distilled wisdom. Which made me ask myself, do we only rely on our own experiences to teach us lessons in life? I know I do, or should I say I did at one point in time. Trust can be a very awarding feeling if reciprocated and given to people who vale such an emotion.

"The balance of being you is judged by your actions and thoughts"

"Doing nothing is better than doing something wrong"

"Don't get accustom to enduring pain – especially when you don't have too"

For a long time, I did not trust anyone or anything in spite of being hurt by so many people. It wasn't until I adopted another ideology in my life, which changed my perspective, on how I begin to trust others. First, I had to learn how to trust myself. I had to learn how to rely on myself. I did this by holding myself responsible for every action that occurred in my life – past and present. If I had the urge to steal something, I would ask myself "why do you want to steal that item?"

As crazy as it sounds, trust has a lot to do with property and faith. Like having trust in a company to fix your car and not break your transmission and charge you out the ass. Or trusting in a company employee to make your cheese burger with way you like it and be polite to you at the drive-thru window. Trust is something we see every day of the week. The power of trust can change your life you allow it to. Who can you count on when all the chips are down?

Hurting Yourself

As a prison peer mentor at D. R. D. C. in Denver, CO, I've heard a countless amount of life stories from inmates. Some of these stories were very shocking to hear, but none quite as odd as this guy named Jeff. Jeff was a 24-year-old guy who had been sexually abused by his own mother at the early age of 12-years-old. Upon hearing this I was somewhat caught off guard and forced to regroup. Sitting across from him seemed odd, listening to how he described the acts of perversion his mother did to him. He said on his 13th birthday, his mother told him to come lay with her in the bed. She cried on his shoulder for two hours straight before falling fast to sleep. He said it was moments like that which made him feel sorry for her in some odd way. Feelings of confusion, abandonment, and need were what he felt for her.

He said when she died from cancer five years later it made him mad and brokenhearted at the same time. He said he felt mad because he felt as if she had abandoned him, and he was brokenhearted because he felt as if he no longer had a purpose in life.

I sat there emotionless as he told me how after her death he started experimenting the different drugs and contemplating suicide. I felt empathy for him, as I followed his journey of pain.

Asking myself, how could I help him or better yet show him how to help himself. The only thing that came to mind was simply just being a listening ear without judgment.

Our minds are affected by so many different things; therefore, we must be on constant guard of our emotions. Hurt causes us to feel certain way, which sometimes blinds us to the fact of reality. Sometimes the hurt is so severe in our lives, that we create illusions of grandeur as a way of protecting ourselves. Our unconsciousness is similar to our white blood cells which were designed to protect us from things that try to harm our bodies.

"Negatives are like positives, but one you enjoy – the other you scorn"

Hurt People – Hurt People

The Player

In high school I had a reputation of being a lady killer, which was true, but I didn't start off like that. I used to be quite gullible when it came to giving my heart to young women. My change came when a girlfriend of mine left me for an older guy who was headed off to college. I remember being so hurt and disappointed as it tried to call her. She didn't even pick up the phone, but her mother did – telling me her daughter no longer wanted to talk to me. I didn't understand what I did wrong to make her throw away our bond like this.

I was confused and truly lost for quite some time. I hated feeling like this; it reminded me of my childhood. Feelings of abandonment, embarrassment, anger, hurt, hate and waves of disappointment.

All these past emotions made me create an alter ego that demonstrated heartless emotions toward females. I wasn't a total scum bag, but I did a lot to make sure I protected my heart. The death of my adopted mother that same year amplified my perspective on this new chapter of my life. I dropped out of high school or better yet, I was expelled that year for assaulting another student. Hurt People – Hurt People.

As we explore the nature of hurt / harm its best to remember how we react to these things. Life is full of obstacles we must overcome. Overcoming these obstacles on a daily basis gives us a certain level of strength. This same, now imbedded inside of us, acts as a confidence booster for our mentalities. But first we must tale accountability of our hurt and overcome the portrait of our past. I always say the only way to overcome hurt is to overcome it.

Discouraging Advice

Have you ever been excited or fired up about something that you enjoy doing, and out of nowhere someone knocked the wind out of your sail? I can definitely relate to what it feels like to be discouraged by someone in a position of trust.
I remember a guidance counselor one told me in the 8th grade I should inspire to be school janitor because I did not read so well. I told her I wanted to be a lawyer, but she just kept selling me on the whole school janitor bit. So, whenever the summer came around I got a part time job at the school as a junior janitor. The job consisted of seeping the hallways, scraping bubble gum from under the tables, wiping windows, fixing lights, and choking toilets with toilet brushes. That was my life for five months, and I truly hated it. I was very unhappy because I was doing something I knew I had no passion for.

Reflecting back on my guidance counselor's advice, I asked myself how many parents/caregivers push, persuade, or place their children in things the kids have no desire to be in?
Probably a lot more than you think huh!

Giving out Advice

Exposing False Teachers

Better Than Ever

PRINCIPLES

I've learned over the years that it is very important to let people figure things out for themselves. By letting others navigate their own path we grant them the gift of free will. Free will is the power to choose your own destiny in life. The will to empower yourself and motivate yourself helps you gain confidence in your everyday life.

<u>'Accepting Advice'</u>

When accepting advice from others, it is best to ask yourself a few questions.
Is the person giving you the advice truly happy in their entire life?

Does their advice speak to volumes to your inner soul?
Are you satisfied with their advice?

These questions will give you insight and help you accept the advice more fruitfully. On another note always remember; never let anyone steal your thunder. If you believe in something and hold it dear to your heart, please don't allow anyone to tell you how to feel about it.

"Don't forget what it means to be you"

Chapter 9

Time

A Twisted Fate

I remember the first time I met a bully in the 7th grade. He had ragged clothes, a hard scroll, and he was bigger than the entire school. When I say he was bigger than the entire school I mean there were teachers he towered over. As a twist of fate, one day this other kid, the same size as him, transferred to our school. As you may know you can't put two circus bears in the same show without maker the lights brighter. Which means every bully is threatened by anything that has the potential to take his or her place.

These two despised each other with a burning passion from the first glance. It wasn't long before they were dancing in the hallway of our school. I saw a fist flying and heard a bunch of quiet voices when the dust settled. The faces of my fellow students were picture ready as they saw the throne take a sudden shift before their eyes. I personally thought it was quite funny and found myself relieved to see a change of monarchy, in the famous movie 'Demolition Man' there is a line I very much love and remember (send a manic to catch a manic). I believe that is true, but in today's world (not to mention the last 15 years) we've seen something uncannily significant. As a country we've seen the effects of bullying lead to a matter of life and death. This is one of the underlining factors of hurt people hurt people. Imagine the level of anger that settles in their heart. The same anger that makes a child plot, plan, and seek revenge on his or her school mates. In some cases, they seek revenge on the teachers and staff as well.

WHEN CIVILIZATION DIE

I do not think the greatest threat to our future is from bombs, or guided missiles. I don't think our civilization will die that way. I think it will die when we no longer care; when the spiritual forces that make us wish to be right and mobile die in the hearts of men. Nineteen notable civilizations have died from within, and not been conquered from without. It happened slowly, in the quiet and dark, when no one was aware.

Lawrence K. Gould

You know it is truly sad to see the cause and effect that takes place in the mist of tragedy. It is even more heart breaking to rasp the amount of loss all the families suffer from these tragedies. Consider the after affect that goes along with every loss. I ask myself if I were a victim of such tragedy how I would see life. Would I be scared to go out in public places? Would I have a job? Would I even care about life anymore? Hurt people – hurt people.

THE MAN WHO STRIVES

It is not the critic who counts not the man who points out how the strong man stumbled, or where the doer of deeds could have done better. The credit belongs to the man who is actually in the arena: whose face is marred by dust and sweat and blood who strives valiantly: who errs, and who comes short again and again. It is he who knows the great enthusiasm, the great devotions, and spends himself in a worthy cause: who at best knows in the end the triumphs of high achievement: and who, at the worst, if he fails, at least fails while daring greatly so that his place shall never be with those cold and timid souls who know neither defeat nor victory.

Theodore Roosevelt

"Everyone's tomorrow is waiting for them today"

Who Are You Really Angry At?

As humans we are wired a certain way which makes us function a certain way. Say you're having a bad day already. Your boss chewed you out for something pity, and it upset you. On the drive home you notice the gas meter is almost on empty. You remember your son asked to barrow your car last night, and obliviously did not put gas in the tank. You are disappointed in his lack of care as you drive home. As soon as you get home, you simply want to relax and kick back. But you notice the house has not been cleaned and no one has cooked. You blow up in a ranting rage and start slamming things down.

Who Are You Really Angry At?

I can't tell you how many times I've been mad at something else and allowed it to bleed over to someone else. Like a nuclear reactor I believe we all explode after so much pressure builds up inside of us. Feelings of being misused, or expendable in our everyday lives, especially by the people we care about the most, hurt us. But the underlining factor in this passage points out how anger builds up inside of us. Anger is like a machine fueled by our emotions. Anger causes us to feel out of control, reckless, disappointed, fearful, confused, and a countless of other nasty emotions.

The most agreeable companion – one who would not have you any different from what you are.

The greatest deceiver – one who deceives himself.

The greatest comfort – the knowledge that you have done your work well.

The greatest mistake – giving up.

The three expensive indulgences – self pit, hate and anger

The greatest stumbling block – egotism

The most ridiculous asset – pride

The best teacher – one who make you want to learn.

The meanest feeling – feeling bad at another's success.

The greatest happiness – helping others.

The greatest thing in all the world – LOVE.

How Do I Heal My Anger?

I would say don't worry so much about trying to heal your anger as how to cope with your anger. It is a proven fact that most people get trapped in the paradox of trying to heal the anger – big mistake. Trying to heal your anger would imply you are sick or there's something wrong with you.

Trust me when I say to you anger is not a sickness. The love of anger could be classified as sickness, but not anger itself. Everyone get angry at something at one point in time of their life. Even Jesus loss his temper and flipped over a table of gold coins. Anger is normal to all those who have emotions, and remain true to themselves. But as you explore your anger and grow to understand its truth, feel free to ask yourself, who am I really angry at?

'Find a purpose to smile and love something or someone'.

'If you never open your eyes you'll never see yourself'.

Hoarders of hurt

It's not what you'd do with a million, if riches should your lot, but what you're doing new with the book and a half you've got.

What does it mean to be a hoarder of hurt? It means you have accepted your victim role in life and you act it out to the fullest. It means you're the kind of people who, in some odd way, likes to be hurt. O.k. that's pretty harsh I will admit it's not that you like to be hurt, but you do look forward to being let down by others. More importantly you like whatever feeling you receive from being or playing the victim role. Well I say play time is over for you darting squirrels of pain. It's time to shake the tree and see what falls out of your state of disappointment.

How Can You Help A Hoarder Of Hurt?

> The highest reward a man can receive for his toil is not what he gets for it, but what he becomes by it.
>
> When you've made a fool of yourself, a real friend doesn't feel that you've done a permanent job.
>
> The blossom cannot tell what becomes of its odor, and no man can tell what becomes of his influence and example, that roll away from him, and go beyond his ken on their perilous mission.
>
> *H. W. Beecher*

Chapter 10
of

Agenda

(Yelling)

Recently I was blessed to receive a lesson that made me ponder. My son and I were talking about how he no longer desired to play football anymore. At first, I found myself blown away by this motion. Football as a freshman is the cornerstone of a young man's high school years.
Or at least in our family it used to be.
I asked he why he no longer desired to play football?

Ha said 'dad, it's not that I don't like playing football anymore, I just don't like it when my football coach yells at me.'
I instantly flashed back to a time when my football coach yelled at me, and we started arguing in the middle of a game. I can still hear that ass hole yelling my name right now.
'Graham!' he would say at the top of his voice. "If you drop another pass I swear you're going to be riding the bench until mid-season!" I used to suck my teeth with a curse word under my breath.

Anyway, I understood what my son was feeling, and I told him to first talk to the coach before quitting.

People are all wired differently. Some people are motivated by a father figure yelling at them, while others immediately turn their ears off when you yell at them.

I remember a dear friend of mine telling me a story of a few year ago about his father who yelled all the time.

He said as a child he considered his father to be one of the most barbaric individuals he had encountered in his lifetime. He said his father would stumble through the front door and already be cursing like a sailor. The stench of hard liquor soaked into his clothes and resting on his breath. Stating his father's yelling could be heard three doors down from their house.

He said one night his father came in his room to start a fight with him, which resulted in his father breaking two of his ribs.

He told me he never forgave his father for doing that to him. Even when his father laid on his death bed years later and requested to see him – he denied his father the joy of saying he was sorry.

Years later he said he was outside a bar and got into an argument with this guy and broke his nose.
I asked him why?

He said the guy started yelling at him, and he had a flashback of his father (he was still mad at his father).
I think he was mad at himself as well if you ask me.

'We hold on to the things that hurt us for years, telling ourselves we are finding our way, but you know the truth'

Lying***

Most people look at lying like a small blunder but lies have the power to hurt as well. You think they do not? When you consider the little girl, who waits for her alcoholic father to take her to the park, but he never shows up.

Or maybe she begs her father to attend her dance recital, and he blows her off to go watch a football game at a local bar. Say she's walking home from her dance recital, which she feels she performed poorly at, only to look in the window and see her father having the time of his life in the bar.

She feels betrayed by the first man she has ever loved. What if this affects her future relationships to come, and truly discourages her from pursuing a dancing career?

She develops an unseen hate for her father that lingers deep in her heart for many years to come.

At times we feel that lies are harmless, but a closer observation would reveal the truth.

Lies have the power to affect people's emotions in a way that causes hurt, disappointment, disbelieve, doubt, anger, selfishness, spitefulness, and many other harsh emotions.

"If you have to create your life through lies – you're not living one"

Support***

Despite what you may feel support is a very vital thing in a person's life.

You can help or hurt people by your choices to support them or not. I know it seems kind of crybaby(ish) but it is a real thing to keep an eye on.

To help you with the state of their thoughts, just remember some people do not have the inner sources of strength that you may have naturally. So, they might need your support / your inner strength to help them overcome an obstacle.

Who knows the person could be the next Jerry Rice in a raw form, and your support could pay off in your later years.

"We are all stronger together"

Just Change

If someone hits you or your brothers, make sure you hit them back (laughing).

These were the lasting words of my caregivers growing up.

I'm sure they didn't mean any harm b giving me this sound advice, but the effect outweighed the motive.

As a wise person once said, "some of the worst things are done with greatest intentions."

It wasn't long before some kids got it in their heads at school to pick on my younger brother. I spared no expense on their face lifts as I punched them over and over again.

It felt good too. I felt empowered by my actions.

Defending my brother gave me a sense of purpose and identity.

I was the protector of our family. The one nobody wanted to mess with, and it was lovely.

But as we take a good look at the pattern created by a little advice, we see a grand picture.

Anytime someone in my family had a problem I was the first person they would call. The problem with that is I got in trouble a lot.

Plus, I felt like I had to constantly out do myself when it came to demanding my respect from the people who would try to go up against me.

It wasn't long before I would take it too far, and truly hurt someone badly.

This action landed me in the county fail for assault on school grounds. I also was expelled from multiple schools in my younger days.

I know you probably ask why didn't I just stop?
I wish life was that easy My Friends (My reply)
Started speaking for me, so the more I tried to tone down my actions the more guys challenged me.

I was trapped by my own way of life.

It took many years of change to paint a picture for guys to accept as truth. The truth was I had changed for the better. The ones who really wanted better for me were the first to accept my state of change.

But it remained a fact that I was still strong and not weak.

Love is Not Real

These were the words of my best friend, Steve, who looked up at me from a country hospital bed. With a bullet lodged in his chest, he knew the outcome was grime.

As I sat there beside his bed I couldn't help but wonder by none of his family members weren't there? It was kind of sad. He told me some very profound things that I took as sound advice.

He said, "people are very selfish when it comes to showing togetherness."

I just listened as he explained.

Saying "no matter what people say, there all just out for self."

"They will tell you that whatever they're doing is from the heart, but even that is a lie."

I said, "why is that?"

Paying Attention

He said "I do everything for my family, but they could careless

I'm about to die!"

I could tell he was getting upset with his situation.

With tears in his eyes I felt the hurt in his heart.

I believe people hurt each other without notice of their actions.

It is our nature – right?

Or is it?

For a long time, I was confused when people said the word "love" to me.

I had to learn how to love.

When you look at your love ones, ask yourself a real question, do they really love me?

Do they even know what true love consist of?

Many people feel they know what love is but are sadly mistaken about the truth of love.

It's easy to love someone when everything is going good. The champagne life.

But who sticks around when things are at their worst?

I have abandonment issues so personally I hate people who come around when things are good but take off running when things are bad.

I understand that is one of my fray triggers I need to work on, but I struggle with that.

Hurt People – Hurt People

A Quiet First

I remember dating this beautiful girl with hazel brown eyes. She had a very calm demeanor about herself that I grew to admire. The strangest thing about her was she spoke in a very low voice. She spoke as if she was afraid to use her voice. At first, I thought that's just how she was, until one day I had the pleasure of meeting her father. The pleasure was all his as I got a clear picture why she talked so low. Her father was the kind of guy who cut her down with his words.

"Can't you do anything right?"

You're beautiful

"Be smarter than you look?"

"Hold your breath and grow like a flower."

I don't know what that last saying even meant. I just knew it sounded hurtful when I heard it. I remember thinking to myself what would make a man talk to his daughter like this? As I explored into her family tree I notice how deeper the roots became. I met her grandmother, who only stood 5 feet two inches, but made her son seem the size of a worm. She talked to him worse than he talked to his daughter. My first thought was these people are "The Adams Family." Crazy as a pit of road lizards!

Then I notice how people who have been hurt, tend to hurt others as well. I also realized how quick I was to paint her father in a bad light. But after I got a grand view of the whole situation it made me see things from a different set of eyes.

Hurt People – Hurt People

Sexual Abuse

Everyone has pain. Everyone suffers from the hurt of others. Sexual abuse is something that causes scars as well as hurt.

I have never suffered from sexual abuse myself, but I feel a certain type of empathy for the people who suffered such abuse.

Some of my best friends told me how sexual abuse affected them in their earlier years.

So, this part of the book is dedicated to them.

You guys are warriors beyond words. True fighters in my eyesight, and I take my hat off to all who wake and say "I'm no one's victim . . . I'm me."

True strength is what you do when life happen to you.

Love

As we revisit the subject of love, it's best to ask ourselves (what is love?)

Some would say love is the affection we have for someone of inner most feelings.

Others would say there are many forms of love, which have their own instinctive natures.

I say blah, blah, blah, blah, blah, blah.

Which means I believe most people don't know the real essence of love.

Let me make that clearer / I believe half of the people who mutter the word love have no clue what it truly means.

Love, in my opinion, is the fastest way to hurt someone if you break their hearts. They almost never forget what you did to them.

Some of you know exactly what I'm talking about right now, seeing how you probably have someone you still have ill feelings for. All because they hurt you.

"I always say love is like a chess match, and no one wants to lose."

I Love you,

Nothing will ever get in the way of that, because together we have the strength to look the world in the eye and say 'Give us your best shot. We can take it,' and you know what? The world will see that what we have, 'different' thought it may be, is far too beautiful, far too big to ever weaken. You are half of my heart, and I am half of yours. There's no one and nothing that can separate us. We have an awesome future ahead of us. One that I know we'll face together, hand in hand and heart to heart. Because I love you and you love me back.

I Love you

Because you understand me better than anyone I've ever known... You can make me happy and soothe away my cares with just a touch or a word. I love you, because we have so much fun together whenever we go and whatever we do...

I Love the way you can make me laugh, when I need it the most.

I Love you, because of the dreams, we've built together, the ones we're still working on, and the ones we'll dream up years from now. I love you, because I'm a better person with you by my side . . . You give my life a deeper meaning and purpose. I love you, because you're my world, my everything . . . and that will never change,

Let's Talk

Popularity

In a text message world, where people are so distant from each other, you stand alone. The Talker. Someone who understands the value of human communication. Someone who can put together a decent sentence without using 15 emoji symbols to get your point across. You are that one. But sadly, you ask – how do I get my significant other to express what I desire to hear (not what I desire to read)

The simple answer is CVC (Clear Verbal Communication). Meaning you have to sit your mate down, at a place where limited distraction can be controlled, and express to them your deepest sentiments. Let them know you do not prefer to read their words all the time. Explain how text messages do not have the same impact on you as their divine collection of words. Tell them how much their words mean to you. How important they are to hear. Tell them how their words truly help you in so many ways.

*Ask your mate how they feel about what you just expressed to them.

Warning!
Do not get mad if you are not granted the response you expected. It is not personal.
They are not saying "I do not care for you"

CASH

Hand down I've seen some crazy stuff done in the name of cold cash.

I've seen brother fight brothers, and friends fall out for years over money.

In fact, I recall my two favorite aunts having a major dispute over my grandmother's account.

One of my aunts accused the other one of stealing from her own mother. This sent the family into disarray, seeing how we all took sides with each aunt.

It got so bad between them my aunts were literally bribing me with candy to stay away from the opposing aunt.
(I took candy from them both)

They refuse to speak to one another for about seven years. And trust me when I tell you, it got pretty ugly over the years.

That's just my own personal example of how money can divide people, and cause hate/hurt.

I'm sure you have your own accounts you can attest to over money.

Are you at odds with a family member or friend over money now?

If so I understand what you are going through, and I would like to add, life is short.

Enclosing if we were to ask ourselves how does the power of a piece of paper have this effect on us, what do you think the answer would be?

Greed!

No matter what it is, just know money is money.

Hurt People – Hurt People

Unfinished Works

This passage is for all you workaholics out there,
The once who can't sit around the house on the weekend,
and just chill out.

I know you are providing for your love ones, trying to give
them the best life possible.

But sadly humans are complicated. We need love, attention,
affection and support.

Let me guess, you got the promotion you've always wanted,
but it takes away precious time away from your family.

Your daughter seems like she hates you for no reason at all,
and your son gets stranger every time you speak to him.

You are losing contact with your family - I get it.
Not to add your significant other is begging dog – like for
some special attention in the bedroom.

You have to be up early in the morning and don't have to
play around with the bed rails. You are focused.

Once again, I get where you'll coming from, but here me out
for one second.

You could be hurting someone very close to you by neglecting them, and their feelings.
Just like the board rooms, your family needs you.

Plus, it would do you some good to relax every now and then.

A Time For Everything (I don't mean to brush them off)

THE
HAPPINESS
TEST

1 SOUND
SLEEP

Sleep is a very vital state of peace. Try to relax and get some decent sleep. It will make more sense in the morning.

2 FOOD

What goes in the body is the fuel that helps the way you think and react in life.

3 CAREER

A healthy career is something we all desire to have. Just remember to enjoy the times as they come and go.

4 CONNECTION
WITH OTHERS

Others give us purpose in our lives, they are our inner peace. Don't look yourself in a room away from the world.

32%

of people are unhappy in their life.

Remember, if you take of yourself, then you can take better care of others.

Cheating

In 2012, I recall having a cellmate at Sterling Correctional Facility who murdered his wife.

At first, I was blown away how calm he was while discussing such a hard – line subject. He wasn't even normal as he told me how he disposed of her body.

He said he wrapped her up in a sheet and threw her body in the lake beside their house.

(Wow!)

After he finished telling me a detailed story, I couldn't help but ask him why?

He looked me dead in my eyes with a cold stare in his eyes, and simply said "She was cheating on me with my first cousin."

I couldn't say nothing . . . I just shook my head.

Hurt People – Hurt People
The greatest analogy I have ever heard to describe myself came from a female I use to date. I am sure she would not mind me sharing it with you guys.

She said I reminded her of a sail boat.

Describing how at times she found herself deeply envious of my ability to sail my mind away to a private island. Leaving the world behind without care in the least. She told me I created my own problems and solved them by dropping anchors in the water when things gave vice.

Waiting for the perfect tide to come in, so I can go out with it.

She said I took on all storms and battled with the deepest seas known to mankind.

Floating toward the sun. wishing to dock in the heart of someone special.
Forgiving the wind.
Being as I am . . .
A sail boat of time.

Reflecting back on what she told me
I begin to ask myself how could I empower her words?
I did it by understanding and how she saw me.
Telling myself that people see one another in a certain light.
This light is what remains true in the heart and minds of many who know you or get to know you.

Sail on . . . sail on.

Are You a Good Person?

Most people, if not all, go through life with a self – assurance they are good. But I ask myself what does it mean to be good?

Am I good simply because I take care of my family? Or pay my taxes on time? Am I good because I put an extra dollar in the collection plate at church? Am I good because I have a job, and donate to feed the children campaign every month? The answer is no!

Good is not what you do, it's who you are?
God is the state of being better, or well – founded.
Good is something that is taught by your care givers or simply known within.
Don't worry about being good – focus on being you.

ARE YOU A GOOD PERSON?

The Circle of Hurt

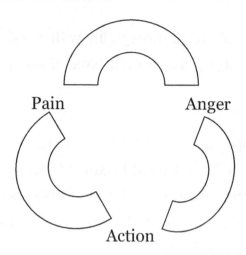

Pain

Anger

Action

In this process you'll find how easy it is to hurt someone or become a victim of one of the three. Keep a watchful eye out.

Fait Accompli

Gracefully taking a bow, I leave you in the light of love.

With thoughts that you have or read here, I encourage you to begin to understand how hurt people – hurt people.

I sent many years causing hurt to others, unaware of my destructive patterns. Once I was made aware of my ways, it was only right I focus my life on being conscious of the effects of hurt.

The accounting principles of this book gave me a divine sense of being. I only hope you guys take care of one another and be very conscious of every emotion with yourself and others.

Thank you for your time, support, and patience.

William S. Graham

Hurt People – Hurt People

William S. Graham is cofounder and CEO of ALOT Foundation (Actually Living Off Talent).

He is also a prominent and intense motivational speaker, a father, a businessman and an author.

Graham speaks to audience from all different walks of life.

At the early age of 19, Graham was convicted of aggravated robbery and sentenced to serve out a 72-year prison bid.

After 15 years in the Colorado Department of Corrections, Mr. Graham emerged a new man with outstanding goals to truly accomplish. The same goals that activated him to put himself in a position to win.

He would like everyone to know if his pain helped just one person, it was well worth it.

Graham would like to thank you guys for supporting his cause and giving him inspirational love.

THE (above) AVERAGE GUY

The Love Locksmith, also by author William S. Graham is available for purchase on Amazon, Barnes & Noble and Google Play!

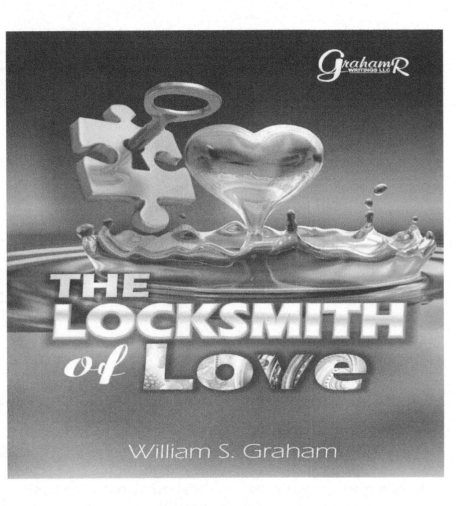

Like" us on Facebook to catch all the latest news on our authors, new works, and all our random giveaways!

www.facebook.com/GrahamRSeries

Connect with us on Instagram & Twitter

Instagram: @GrahamRSeries

Twitter: @GrahamRWrites

Looking to get your work published? Contact us as submissions@grahamrwritings.com!

Made in United States
Orlando, FL
06 April 2024

45536115R00088